CHORAL SIGNATURE SERIES

SATB (divisi)

MORTEN LAURIDSEN

O Magnum Mysterium

AF658714

Morten Lauridsen

FABER ff MUSIC

Morten Lauridsen

Composer Morten Lauridsen is most noted for his seven vocal cycles – *Les Chansons des Roses, Madrigali, Mid-Winter Songs, Cuatro Canciones, A Winter Come, Lux Aeterna* and *Nocturnes* – and his series of *a cappella* motets which are regularly performed by distinguished ensembles and vocal artists throughout the world. His *O magnum mysterium* and *Dirait-on* have become two of the most performed and recorded compositions of recent years. 'Lux Aeterna', a CD of his compositions recorded by the Los Angeles Master Chorale conducted by Paul Salamunovich, was a Grammy nominee in 1998. Morten Lauridsen (b. 1943) is Professor of Composition at the University of Southern California Thornton School of Music and served as Composer-in-Residence of the Los Angeles Master Chorale from 1995–2001. Additional information regarding Morten Lauridsen may be found at mortenlauridsen.com.

A compact disc of Morten Lauridsen's music has also been recorded by Polyphony and the Britten Sinfonia, under the direction of Stephen Layton, for Hyperion (CDA 67449, www.hyperion-records.co.uk).

> *'Layton and company have here produced the finest I've heard among several excellent collections of Lauridsen's work. None are quite as exquisitely nuanced or sung with such glowing vocal sheen as this. Clear and shimmering sound, plus Hyperion's usual complete and user-friendly booklet, make it all the more attractive. No committed choral fan or singer will ever regret letting Lauridsen into his life'.*
>
> (American Record Guide)

This edition first published in 2002 by Faber Music Ltd as exclusive licensee
in UK, Eire, Australia, New Zealand, Hong Kong, Singapore, Malaysia and South Africa.
Bloomsbury House 74–77 Great Russell Street London WC1B 3DA
Music processed by MusicSet 2000
Printed in England by Caligraving Ltd

ISBN10: 0-571-52128-2
EAN13: 978-0-571-52128-9

To buy Faber Music publications or to find out about the full range of titles available
please contact your local retailer or Faber Music sales enquiries:

Faber Music Limited, Burnt Mill, Elizabeth Way, Harlow, CM20 2HX England
Tel: +44 (0)1279 82 89 82 Fax: +44 (0)1279 82 89 83
sales@fabermusic.com fabermusic.com

commissioned by Marshall Rutter in honour of his wife, Terry Knowles, and first performed by Los Angeles Master Chorale, directed by Paul Salamunovich, in Dorothy Chandler Pavilion, Los Angeles, on 18 December 1994

O magnum mysterium

O great mystery, and wondrous sacrament, that animals should see the new-born Lord, lying in their manger! Blessed is the Virgin whose womb was worthy to bear the Lord Jesus Christ. Alleluia!

MORTEN LAURIDSEN

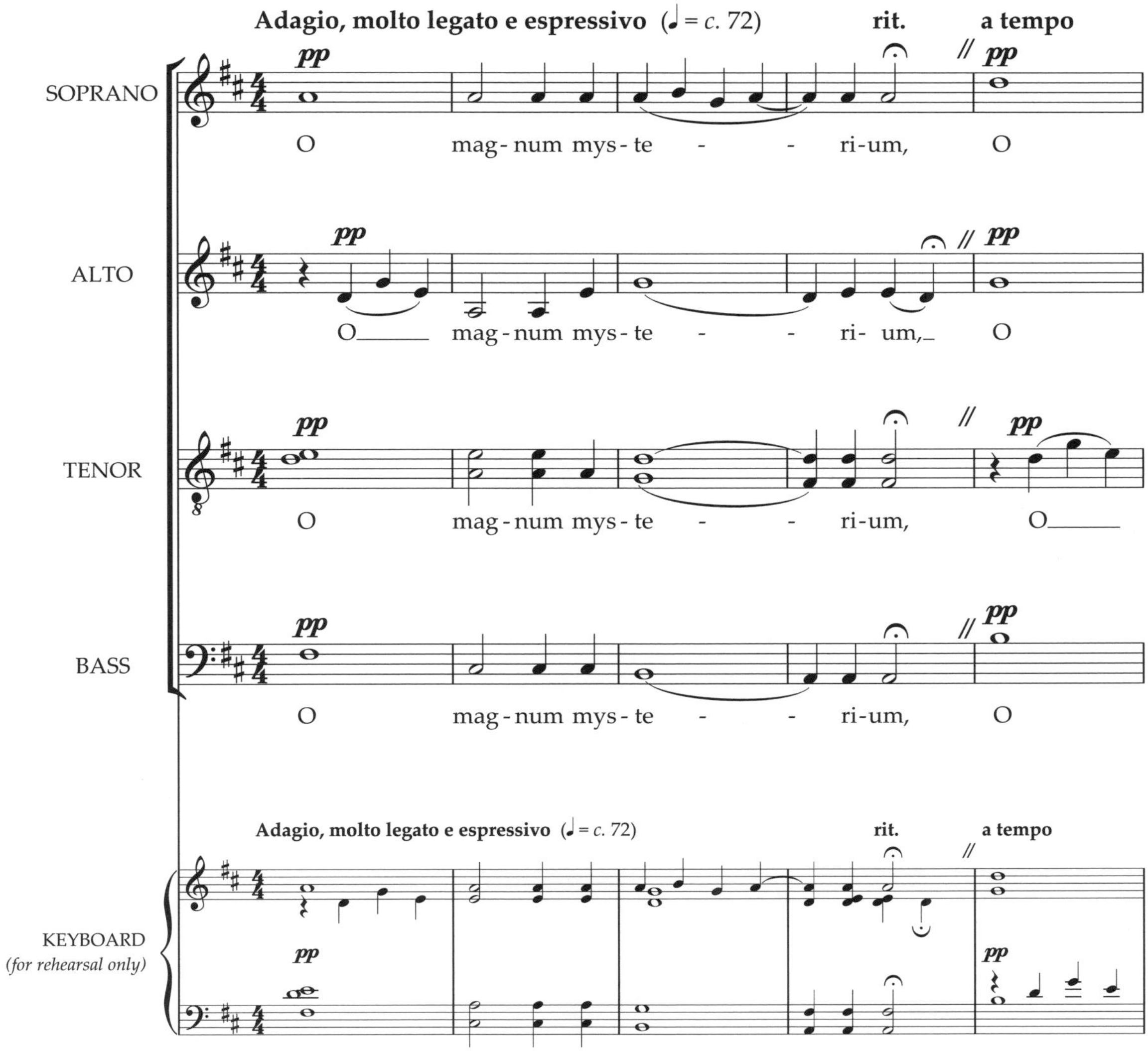

This edition published in 2002 by Faber Music Ltd as exclusive licencee in UK, Eire, Australia, New Zealand, Hong Kong, Singapore, Malaysia and South Africa.

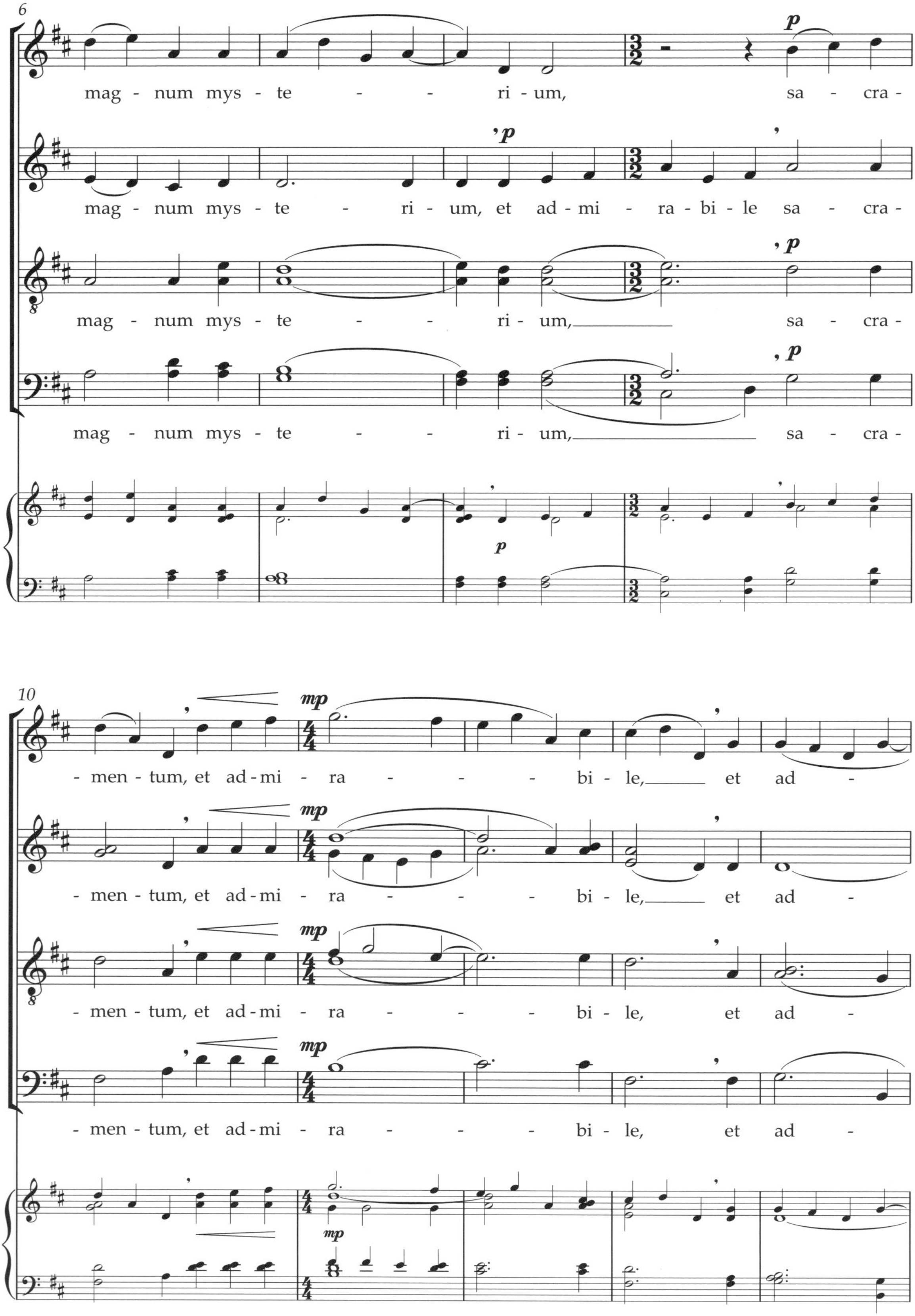
6
p
mag - num mys - te - - ri - um, sa - cra -
'p
mag - num mys - te - ri - um, et ad - mi - ra - bi - le sa - cra -
,p
mag - num mys - te - - ri - um, sa - cra -
,p
mag - num mys - te - - ri - um, sa - cra -
p
10
mp
- men - tum, et ad - mi - ra - - - bi - le, et ad -
mp
- men - tum, et ad - mi - ra - - - bi - le, et ad -
mp
- men - tum, et ad - mi - ra - - - bi - le, et ad -
mp
- men - tum, et ad - mi - ra - - - bi - le, et ad -
mp

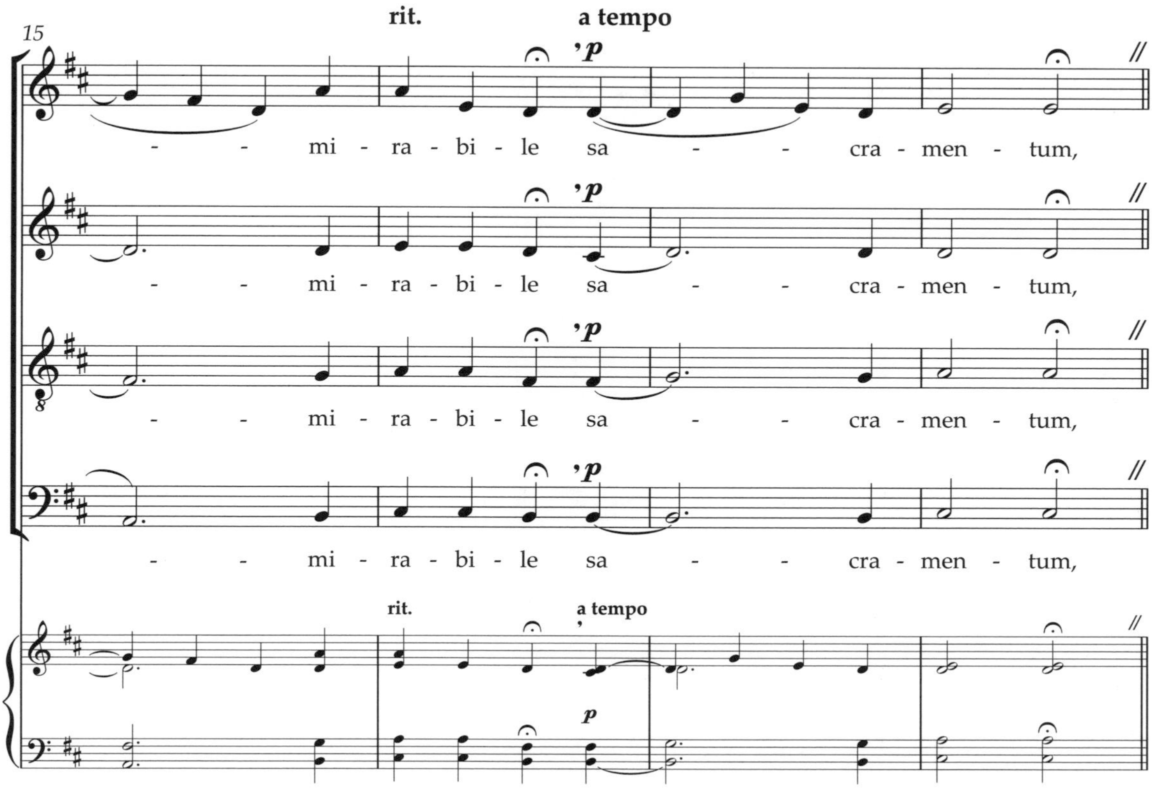
15
rit.
a tempo
- - mi - ra - bi - le sa - - cra - men - tum,
- - mi - ra - bi - le sa - - cra - men - tum,
- - mi - ra - bi - le sa - - cra - men - tum,
- - mi - ra - bi - le sa - - cra - men - tum,
rit.
a tempo

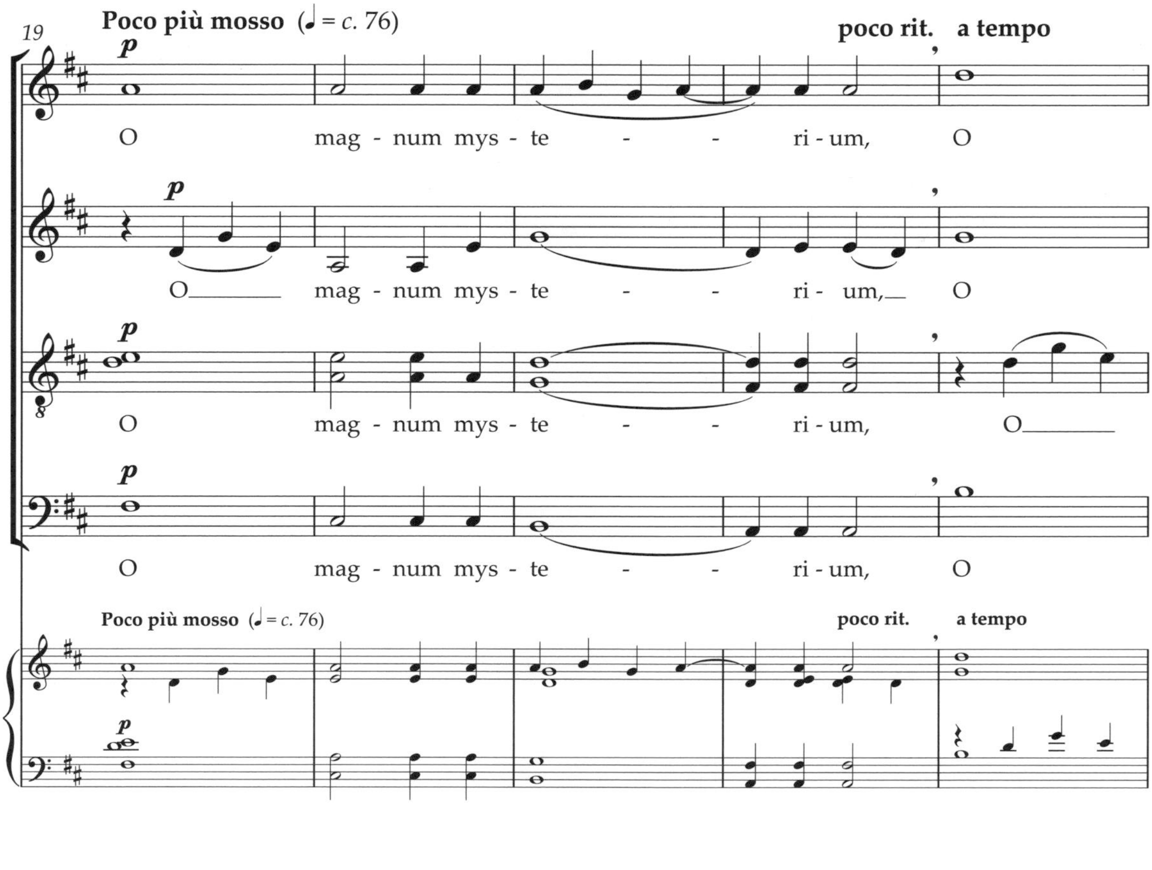
19
Poco più mosso (♩ = c. 76)
poco rit.
a tempo
O mag - num mys - te - - ri - um, O
O mag - num mys - te - - ri - um, O
O mag - num mys - te - - ri - um, O
O mag - num mys - te - - ri - um, O
Poco più mosso (♩ = c. 76)
poco rit.
a tempo

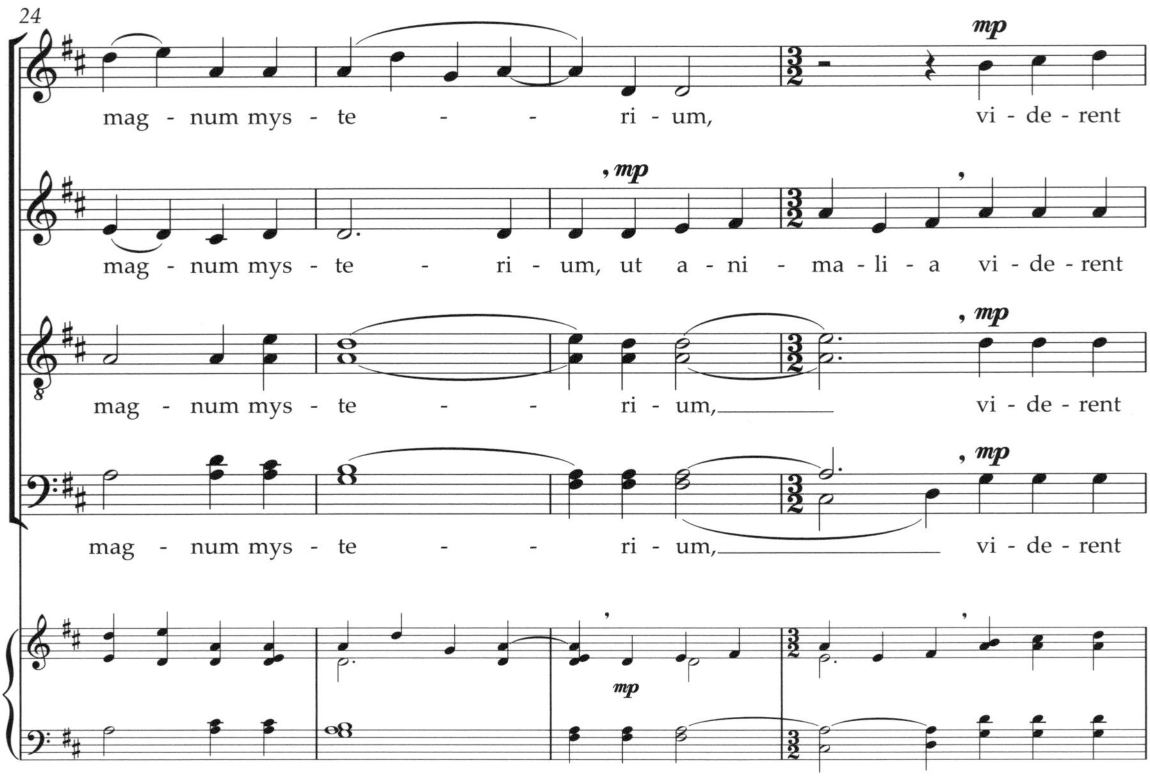
24
mp
mag - num mys - te - - ri - um, vi - de - rent
mp
mag - num mys - te - ri - um, ut a - ni - ma - li - a vi - de - rent
mp
mag - num mys - te - - ri - um, vi - de - rent
mp
mag - num mys - te - - ri - um, vi - de - rent
mp

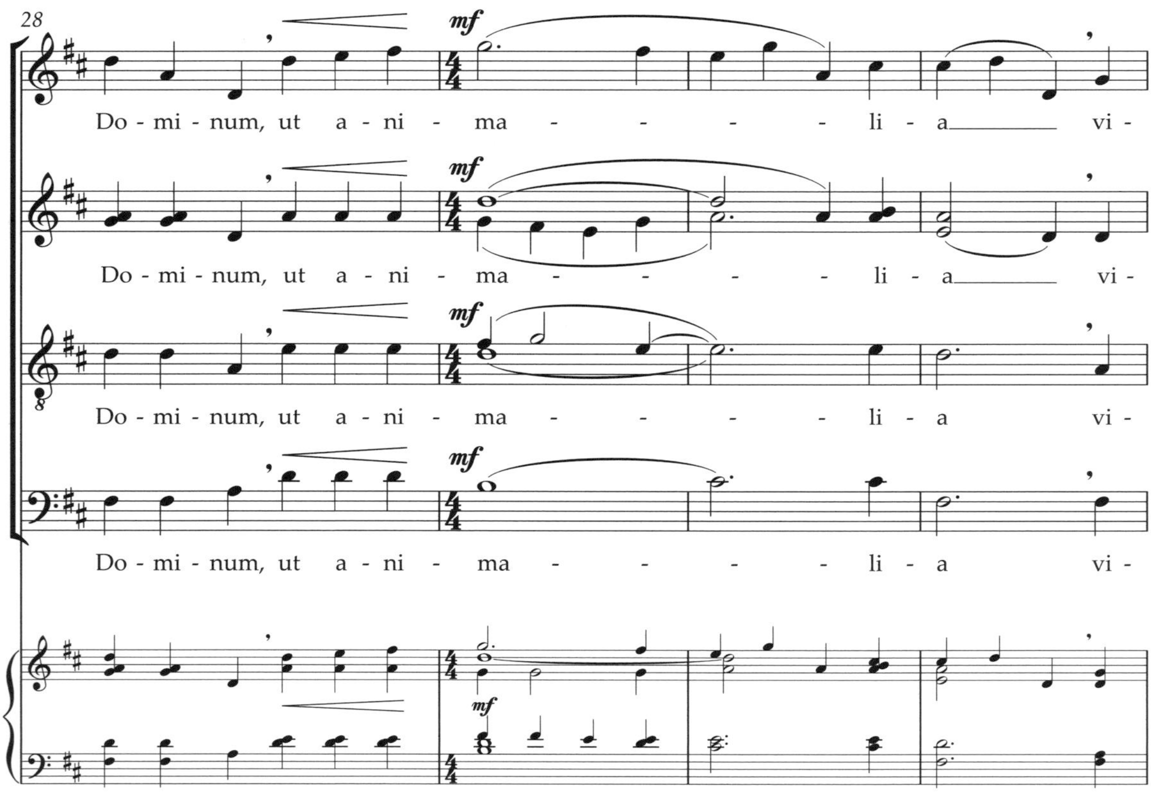
28
mf
Do - mi - num, ut a - ni - ma - - - - li - a vi -
mf
Do - mi - num, ut a - ni - ma - - - - li - a vi -
mf
Do - mi - num, ut a - ni - ma - - - - li - a vi -
mf
Do - mi - num, ut a - ni - ma - - - - li - a vi -
mf

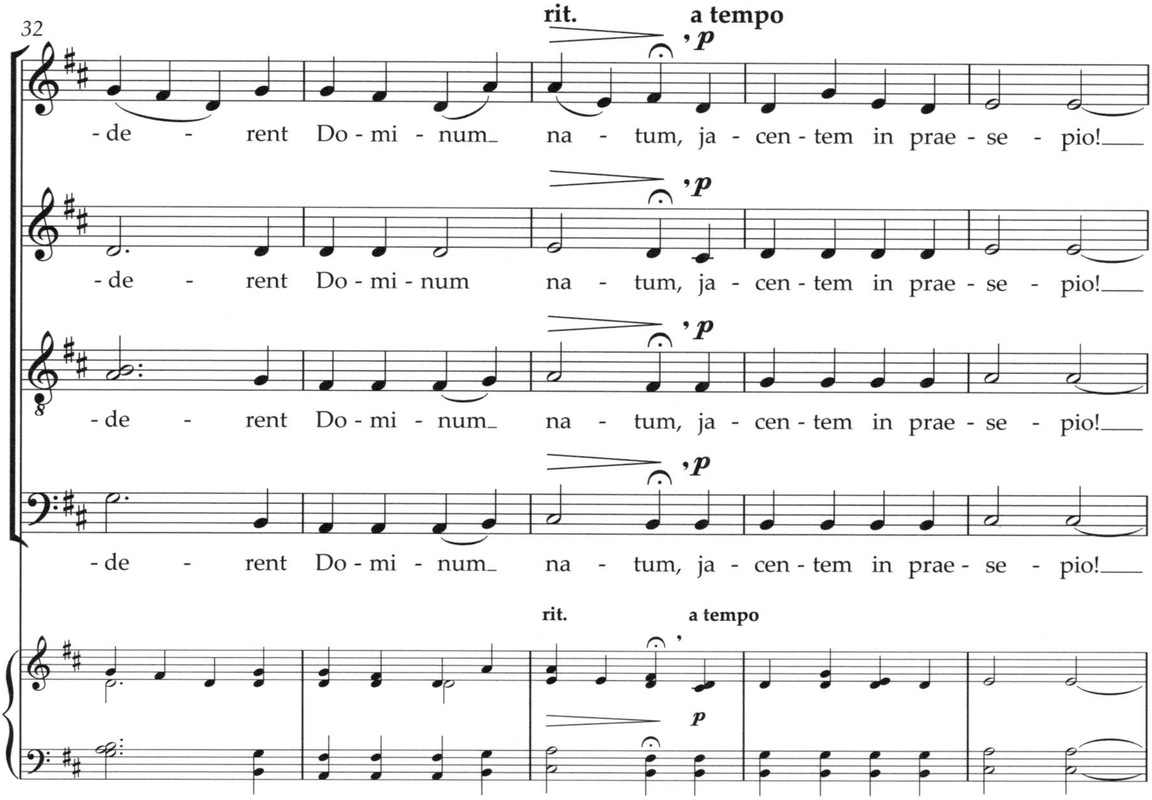
32
rit.
a tempo
p
-de - rent Do - mi - num na - tum, ja - cen - tem in prae - se - pio!
rit.
a tempo
p

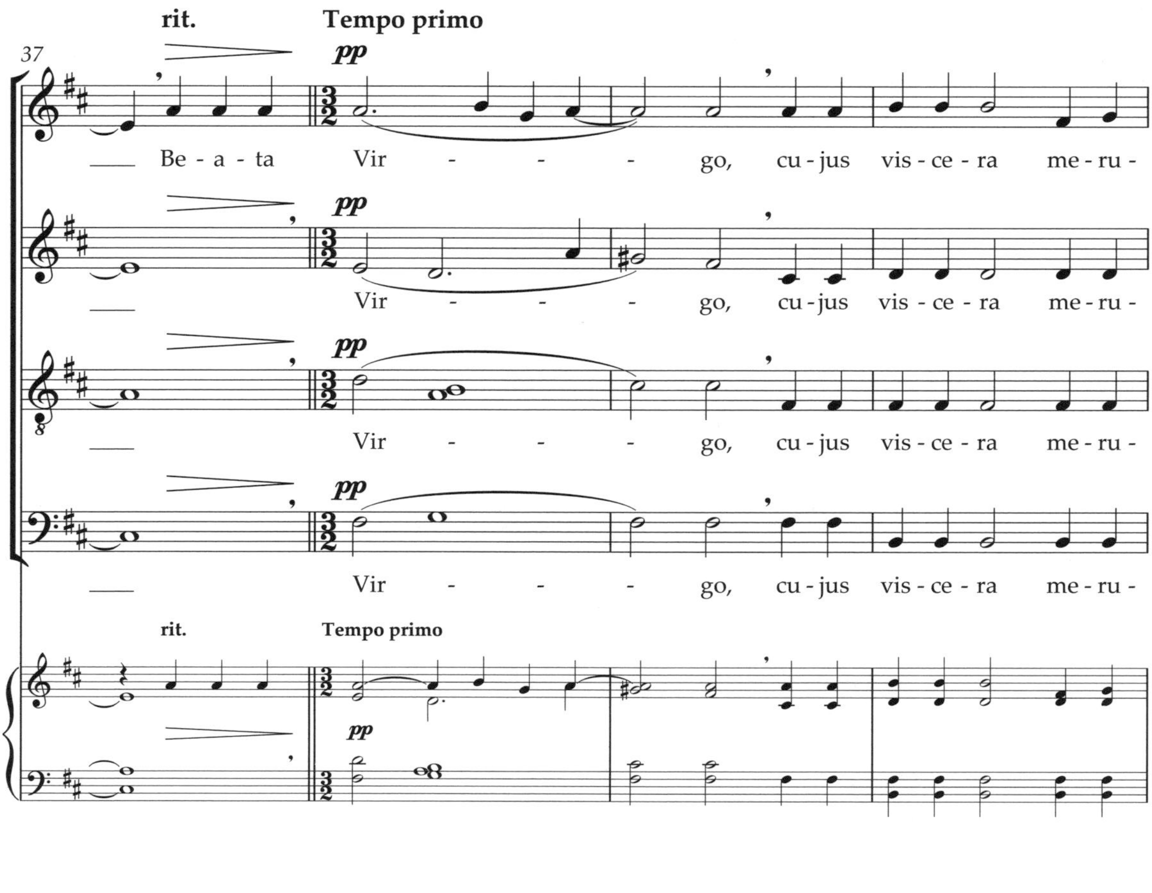
37
rit.
Tempo primo
pp
Be - a - ta Vir - - - go, cu - jus vis - ce - ra me - ru -
Vir - - - go, cu - jus vis - ce - ra me - ru -
rit.
Tempo primo
pp

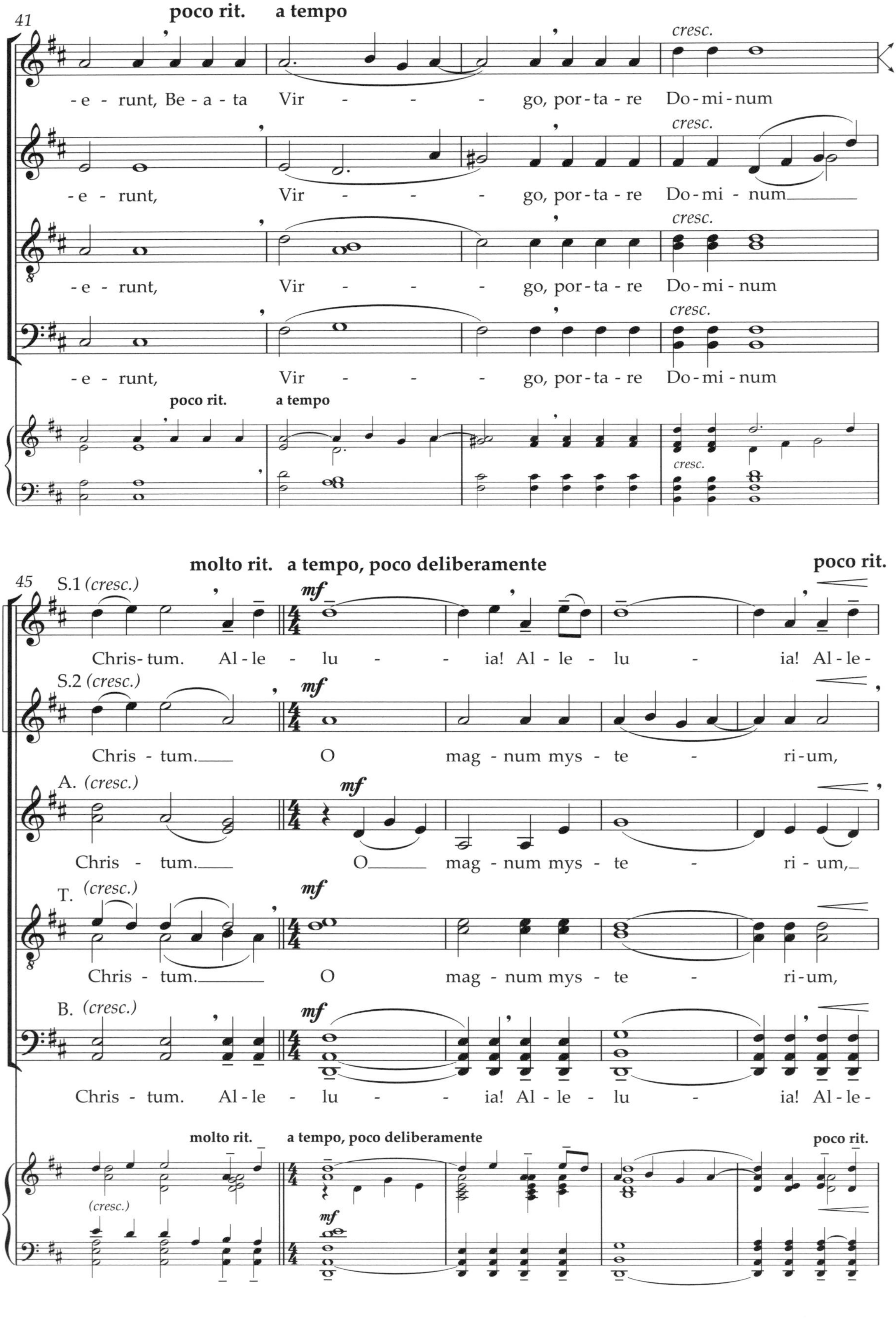
41
poco rit.
a tempo
cresc.
-e - runt, Be - a - ta Vir - - - go, por - ta - re Do - mi - num
-e - runt, Vir - - - go, por - ta - re Do - mi - num
-e - runt, Vir - - - go, por - ta - re Do - mi - num
-e - runt, Vir - - - go, por - ta - re Do - mi - num
45
molto rit.
a tempo, poco deliberamente
poco rit.
S.1 (cresc.)
mf
Chris - tum. Al - le - lu - - ia! Al - le - lu - ia! Al - le -
S.2 (cresc.)
Chris - tum. O mag - num mys - te - ri - um,
A. (cresc.)
Chris - tum. O mag - num mys - te - ri - um,
T. (cresc.)
Chris - tum. O mag - num mys - te - ri - um,
B. (cresc.)
Chris - tum. Al - le - lu - - ia! Al - le - lu - ia! Al - le -

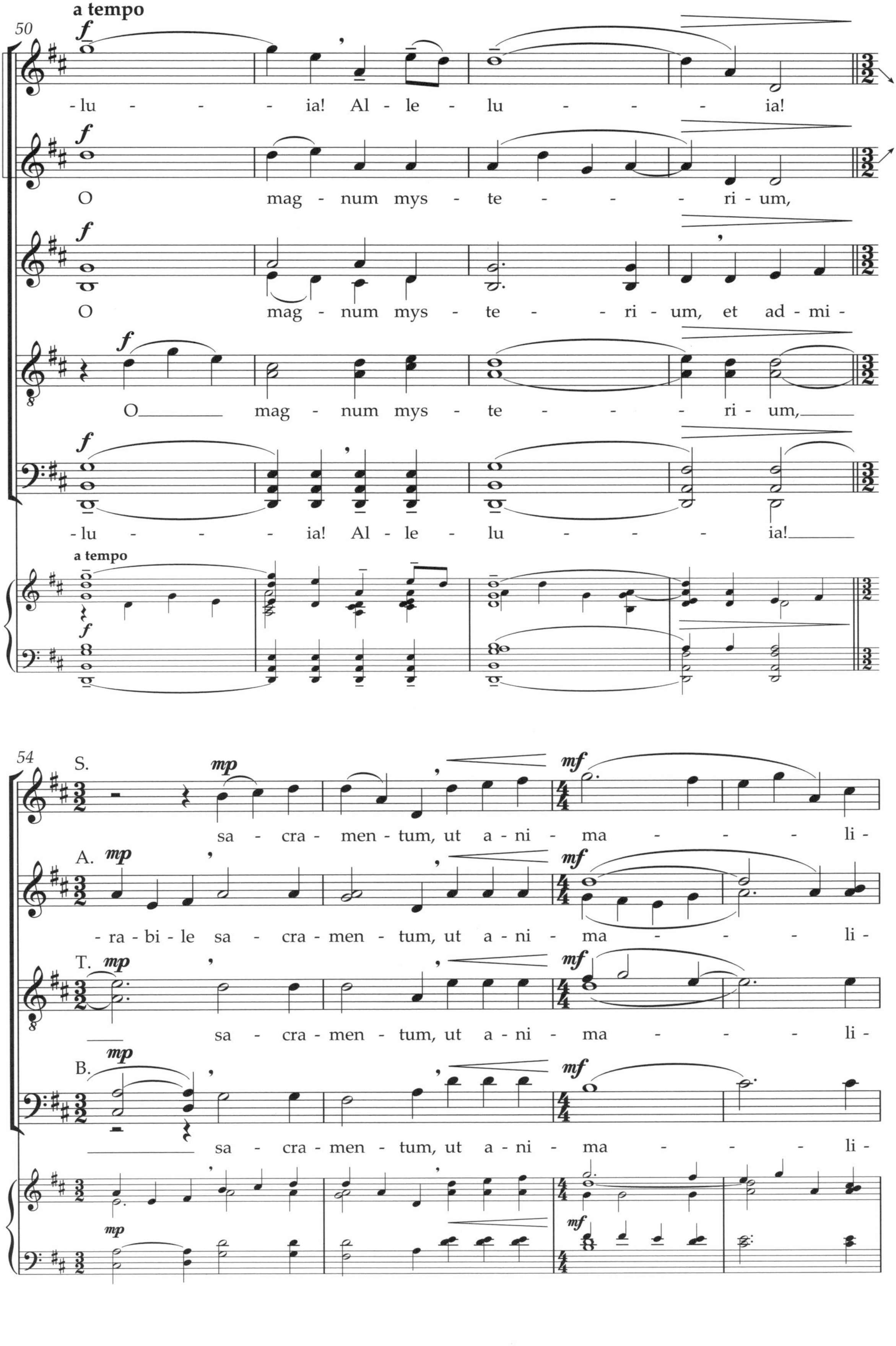
a tempo
50
-lu - - - ia! Al - le - lu - - - - ia!
O mag - num mys - te - - - - ri - um,
O mag - num mys - te - - ri - um, et ad - mi -
O mag - num mys - te - - - - ri - um,
-lu - - - ia! Al - le - lu - - - - ia!
a tempo
54
S. sa - cra - men - tum, ut a - ni - ma - - - - li -
A. - ra - bi - le sa - cra - men - tum, ut a - ni - ma - - - li -
T. sa - cra - men - tum, ut a - ni - ma - - - li -
B. sa - cra - men - tum, ut a - ni - ma - - - li -

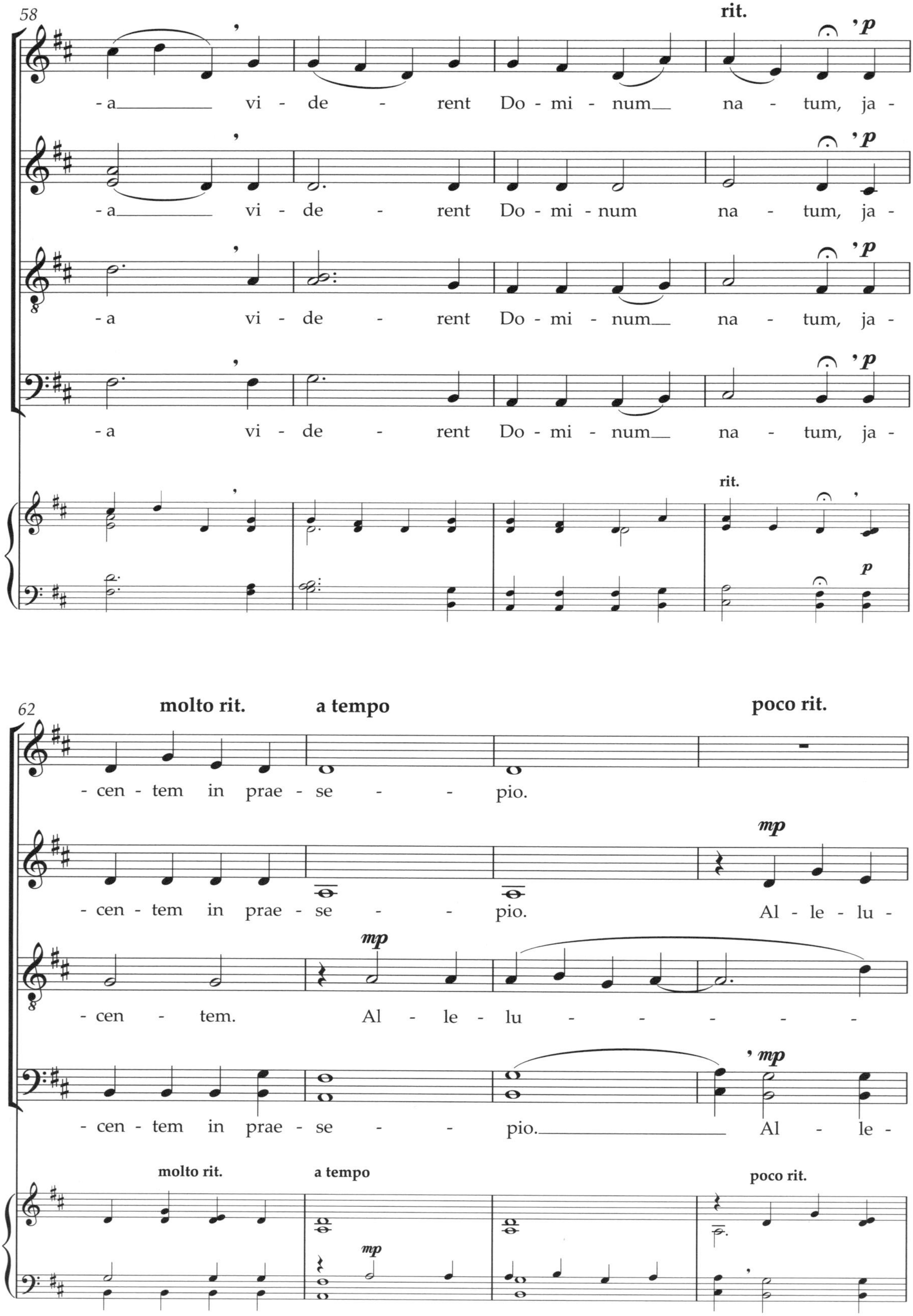
58
rit.
-a vi - de - rent Do - mi - num na - tum, ja -
-a vi - de - rent Do - mi - num na - tum, ja -
-a vi - de - rent Do - mi - num na - tum, ja -
-a vi - de - rent Do - mi - num na - tum, ja -
rit.
62
molto rit.
a tempo
poco rit.
- cen - tem in prae - se - - pio.
- cen - tem in prae - se - - pio. Al - le - lu -
- cen - tem. Al - le - lu - - - - -
- cen - tem in prae - se - - pio. Al - le -
molto rit.
a tempo
poco rit.

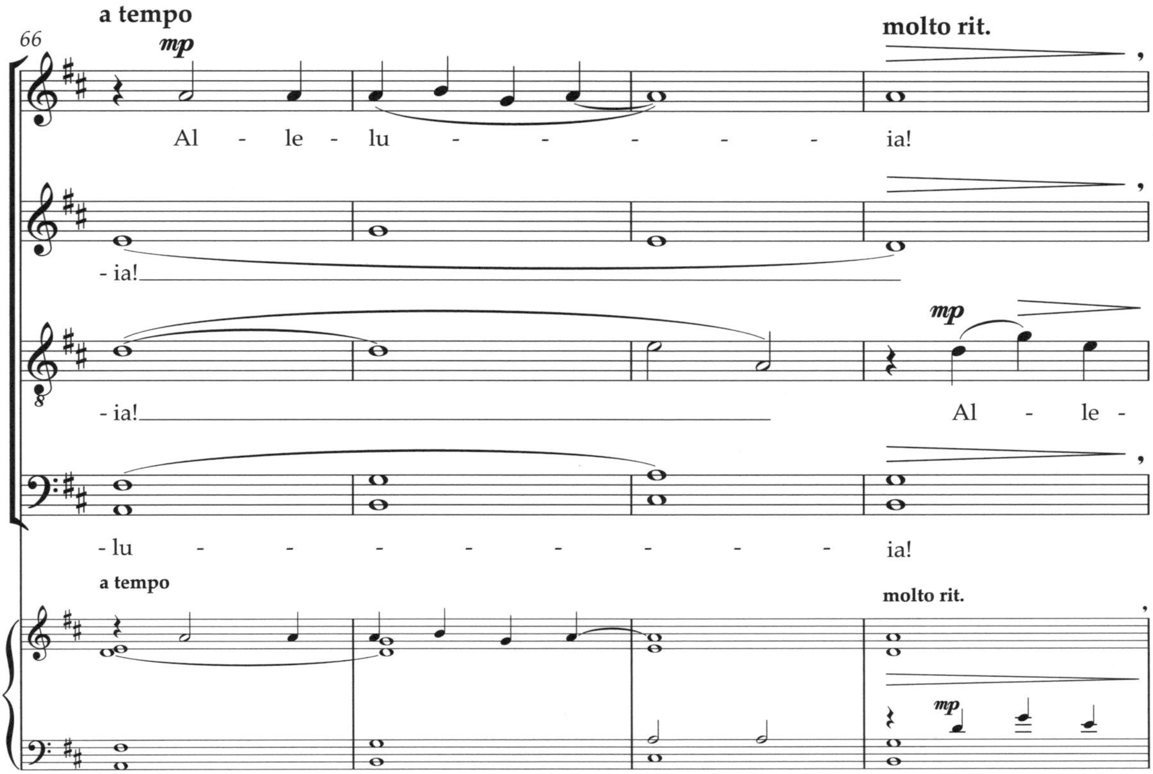

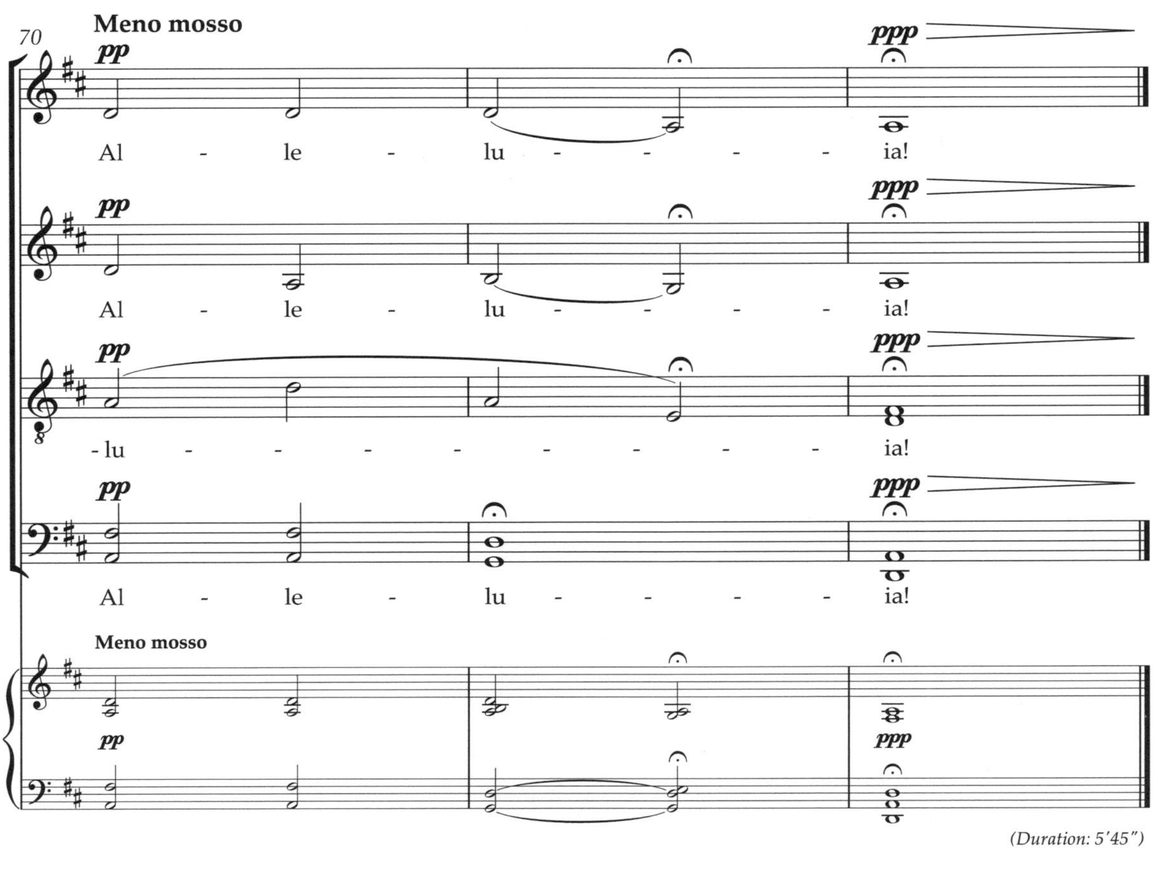

(Duration: 5′45″)

CHORAL SIGNATURE SERIES

Consultant Editor: Simon Halsey

WORKS INCLUDE:

Thomas Adès .... The Fayrfax Carol
.... January Writ
Julian Anderson .... Four American Choruses
Brendan Ashe .... For the Fallen
.... Sanctus
Jonathan Dove .... Ecce Beatam Lucem
.... Into Thy Hands
.... Seek Him that Maketh the Seven Stars
.... Wellcome, all Wonders in One Sight!
.... Who Killed Cock Robin?
Vladimír Godár .... Dormi, Jesu
.... Regina Coeli
Howard Goodall .... In Memoriam Anne Frank
.... Jubilate Deo
.... Lead, Kindly Light
.... The Lord is My Shepherd
.... Love Divine
.... The Marlborough Canticles
.... Spared
Francis Grier .... Alleluia! I Bring You News of Great Joy
.... Two Advent Responsories
Jonathan Harvey .... Come, Holy Ghost
.... Remember, O Lord
Malcolm Hayes .... Corpus Christi
Nigel Hess .... Jubilate Deo
Matthew Hindson .... Home
Morten Lauridsen .... Ave Dulcissima Maria
.... Ave Maria
.... O Come, Let Us Sing Unto The Lord
.... O Magnum Mysterium
.... O Nata Lux
.... Prayer
.... Ubi Caritas et Amor
Alexander L'Estrange ... Lute-book Lullaby
.... On Eagles' Wings
.... Prayers for Peace
Wayne Marshall .... Magnificat & Nunc Dimittis in C
Matthew Martin .... Adam Lay Ybounden
.... Ecce Concipies
Colin Matthews .... The Angels' Carol
Nicholas Maw .... One Foot in Eden Still, I Stand
Peter Sculthorpe .... Morning Song for the Christ Child
John Woolrich .... Spring in Winter

Difficulty Rating ★★☆ moderately challenging

The Faber Choral Signature Series introduces a wealth of new or recently written choral music to choirs in search of fresh repertoire. The series draws in a rich diversity of living composers and includes both lighter and more challenging contemporary works, offering a thrilling array of varied styles.

For centuries, composers have been inspired by the beautiful 'O magnum mysterium' text depicting the birth of the new-born King amongst the lowly animals and shepherds. This affirmation of God's grace to the meek and the adoration of the Blessed Virgin are celebrated in my setting through a quiet song of profound inner joy.

Morten Lauridsen

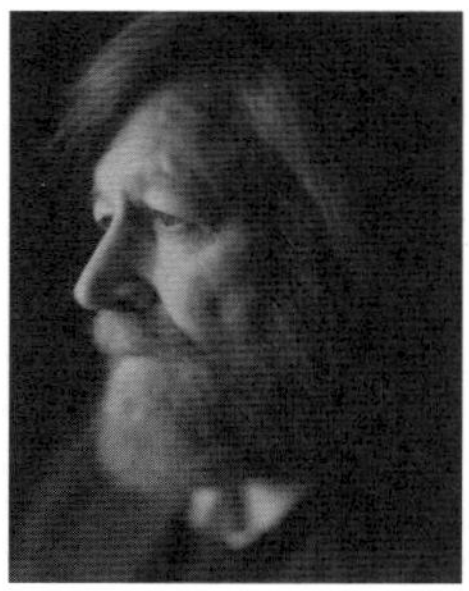

MORTEN LAURIDSEN occupies a permanent place in the standard vocal repertoire of the 21st century. In 2006, he was named an 'American Choral Master' by the National Endowment for the Arts, and in 2007 he was awarded the National Medal of Arts, the highest artistic award in the United States, by the President in a White House ceremony, 'for his composition of radiant choral works combining musical beauty, power, and spiritual depth'.

For a full listing of works, to peruse scores and listen to recordings, go to **www.choralstore.com**

Join our on-line choral community:
www.facebook.com/choralstore **Twitter: @choralstore**

FABER MUSIC
fabermusic.com

ISBN10: 0-571-52128-2
EAN13: 978-0-571-52128-9

9780571521289